BY

JAMES DILLET FREEMAN

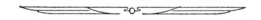

UNITY BOOKS
UNITY VILLAGE, MISSOURI

This is one of a series of Unity books devoted to teaching how you can make your life better by applying Christian principles. The first Unity book, *Lessons in Truth,* was published in 1894 and is still in print. The Unity work itself was established in 1889, when its founders, Charles and Myrtle Fillmore, began to share with others the truth that had helped them.

The Unity movement now reaches millions of persons all over the world. Unity School of Christianity includes the Silent Unity department, to which thousands of people each year write and telephone for prayers for any need, and the Publishing department, which distributes the Unity books and magazines that carry the Unity message around the world. Unity centers and churches are located in many large cities.

Be! was originally published in 1955; seventh printing, 1985.

Art by Ilah Marian Kibbey.

The Way of the Heart

Everyone who writes hopes that what he writes will turn out to be a poem. He does not necessarily want to make words rhyme, but he wants his utterance to be one of truth and beauty and feeling, he wants it to be a beautiful and intense revelation of Truth—and this is what a poem is.

In their noblest moments, in their keenest insights, all men are likely to become poets. It is not just happenstance that the King James Bible is the most beautiful English ever written, or the Koran the most beautiful Arabic, or the Bhagavad-Gita the most beautiful Sanskrit. To express sublime thoughts, the heart cries out for sublime language.

Jesus was a poet. When they asked Him what heaven is, He answered that it is like a mustard seed. That is a poet's answer. When He wanted to show God's

3

relationship to us, He called God our Father. That is a poet's epithet. And there is no greater poem in literature than His Sermon on the Mount.

God might be thought of as a poet. For He was not content to expound abstract principles, but shaped them into the violets, clouds, stars, dew, redbirds, tigers, human beings, and all the rest of the infinite variety of fantastic, noble, original, unique things that form the world.

Many of us are so much a part of life that we take no time or thought to listen to what life has to say to us; we simply live. But some are listeners. They have time (or take time) to stand on a corner of the world and listen—to what the wind has to say in such a hurry, or the tree so patiently, or the cloud so briefly, or the flower in the wall, or the city street, or the people—oh, the lovely, beloved people!—or the still small voice within.

The poet is a listener. Everything is the speech of God, and the poet is His interpreter. The poet listens and puts down what he hears. He listens without prejudice. He is as much concerned with what a mouse has to say as with what the President has to say or with what the Great Nebula in Andromeda has to say. A mouse spoke to Bobbie Burns one day when he was plowing a field, and we are still reading—two hundred years later—what Burns wrote down.

Most of us are tied up in the logic of our own thinking; we have preconceived notions as to what things are and what can be expected from them. Not so the poet. He perfects his techniques, but he leaves his mind free, and he has a hospitable mind. He invites the truth, and expects the unexpected.

This is one of the great joys of writing poetry. I do not dictate to my mind what it should say. I leave it free, and I am often as much surprised at what I have to say as any reader is. A poem is as unpredictable as lightning.

Poetry is the lightning of God. Like the observer in the crow's nest of a ship, the poet has learned to see by lightning. And he speaks by lightning too, in lines and phrases rather than at length. If he writes a long work, it too comes by bursts and flashes; later he arranges these in orderly sequence. A single phrase of poetry may sometimes say more than many pages of prose; a single line as much as a book.

We think we live in an age of prose. But I have noticed that in a time of need, it is likely to be some line of poetry that rises to our mind—perhaps a line we learned by heart in school and thought we had forgotten years before. It is by heart that we have to learn poetry, for poetry is the way of the heart.

Poetry is as intense as life. The wind is not flat, the sea dull, love colorless, God an abstraction—we experience life keenly, with all our faculties. And poetry, like life, is vivid, colorful, concrete. It makes the truth stand out in sharp relief.

Poetry has more dimensions than prose. God is not just a truth you can think about, He is a faith you can feel, a presence you can experience. Poetry enables you to feel and experience God as well as think about Him. The poet does not so much want you to say, "Now I see what God is"; he wants you to say, "Now I see God!"

Prose produces light, but poetry strikes fire—and to live, we need fire! We need the fire of faith, the warmth of love. That is why metaphysics should be poetry. When it becomes poetry, it not only helps us to understand, it helps us to live, it helps us to be.

That is why whenever I sit down to write I pray that what I write may turn out to be a poem—that is, an intense and beautiful revelation of truth. I believe God is. I believe that His Spirit is in man. I believe that faith and love and prayer are life. Because I hold these truths passionately, I want to express them eloquently, for I want you too to hold them passionately. I want you to know them not only in your mind but with every fiber of your being. I want you to *be* these truths. I believe that they are life to you.

CONTENTS

Be!

Be!

We live in an age when many feel that life is meaningless. The skeptic looks at things and sees no reason for believing; for every reason he has a counter-reason.

But life answers the skeptic where reason may not. For life says to him: *Live! Be!*

We do not need speculation to prove that life has meaning, any more than we need a discourse on the laws of light to prove that a rainbow or a sunset has meaning.

Asking the reason for life is like asking the reason for a crocus or love. Life needs no reason for being. It is its own reason for being.

The meaning of music is not to be found in a music book. To find the meaning of music, we have to listen to music —and even then, we may not be able to put its meaning into words. Music has a meaning that words are often inadequate to express.

13

Life is like music. Its Composer had a thought for which words were inadequate. So He said, simply, "Let there be!" All the music of life is the expression of His thought.

We may not have found God, but that does not mean that He is not there. We may not be able to work problems in calculus, but they can be worked. We do not have to know the answer to know that there is an answer.

Outside my window a redbird fills the morning with its singing. It does not sing because it knows the answer. Its song is the answer. Above me a squirrel flings itself from bough to bough. It does not leap because it knows the answer. Its leap is the answer. The rosebush in my garden unfolds a perfect rose. It does not produce the rose because it knows the answer. Its rose is the answer.

Life cries to me with ten thousand thousand tongues that it is meaningful. Morning cries it with sunlight and bird songs and pink rosebud clouds. Noon cries it from a brazen mouth of fire, evening with the still small voice of quietness, night with darkness and the lights

14

of all the stars. Spring shouts it like a hallelujah chorus. The horns of summer blow it across the groves and meadows. Fall's gold and scarlet fifes repeat it on the burning hills. It rumbles on the drums of winter under the brooding snows. Storms cry out its meaning no less than tranquil seasons do.

Every blade of grass crackles it out like a wireless, pushing up under my feet. Every seed affirms it, the sound of the cracking of shells and the splitting of husks, the thud of fruit dropping on the earth, the silence of the tree bare to the winter wind. Mole underground, eagle in the air, striped tiger, horned rhinoceros, squeaking mouse, cawing magpie—all the infinite menagerie of God informs me that life has meaning, a meaning vast and wonderful, beautiful and strange as the world of forms itself.

O the crack-crowding, heart-warming, death-destroying wonder of life! the swarming, sprouting, growing, proliferating wonder! It drifts to and fro in the air. Every inch of earth is packed with it. Let the merest rain fall, and the desert blooms. In the darks of ocean, it abounds.

15

I sense that there is nothing that is not unique, special, important, meaningful. The smallest particle is power incarnate. There is no atom, no merest speck of life that is not pregnant with all the possibilities of the universe. There is so much meaning in the least living thing that its obliteration (if this were possible, which it is not) would make such a void in the heart of God that infinity would be swallowed up in it.

Yet all this world of forms, wrought with such cunning that no two atoms in it are the same, is only the shadow of the wonder and beauty that are there. Strip away the wonder of form and a yet greater wonder appears. For the world of forms that stretches out around us, shifting, fair, new, strange, familiar, passing, passionate, is not dense and corporeal but in reality a world of light. At the heart of all that is, there is fire. We live in a world of light. We are ourselves light. If the many seem wonderful, how much more wonderful is the One! Are you the least? You are no less than the greatest. Even

16

"the least of these" is God.

I have only to look, I have only to reach, I have only to taste, I have only to feel, I have only to live—to know that the world is a work more wonderful than anything I can imagine it to be, anything I do imagine it to be! The wildest wonderment of all poets, dreamers, inventors, speculators that have ever lived is as nothing compared to the wonderment that is the world. The world is God's wonderment, infinite intelligence compounding its infinity, the joy of eternity delighting in itself.

And when I consider man, his dreams and deeds, the deeps in him, the heights in him—frail as flesh, fragile as mind and spirit, yet challenging darkness, even death; not sure of his way but venturing forward, not unafraid but not turning back, not free from pain but with faith that he can master it, not beyond selfishness yet struggling to subdue self; falling yet keeping the vision, loving life yet able to love truth more than life—then it is as if I stand upon a storm-swept plain at night, and suddenly, the clouds split, and behold, the lightning of God! For when I consider man, I catch a glimpse of Him in whose image man is made.

Listen to life, and you shall hear the voice of life crying, *Be!*

What shall you be?

Be what you were made to be!

You were made to be alive. You were made to be joy. You were made to be a son of God. God made you in His image. The impress of His Spirit is on your every living cell.

For this alone all things were made: to be! Life is not to be explained in terms of aims and ends and goals, but only in terms of living. Life has goals and a goal, but its meaning and worth do not depend on this fact. How shall we explain life in terms of ends? There is no end that is not a starting point.

Is it wonderful to be a grown man or woman? It is also wonderful to be a child. The joy of arrival is great, but so is the joy of the journey.

Life is made up of wonderful differences and different wonders; all of life is wonderful. Let us not say of one that it

18

is more or less than another, but let us find meaning and worth in all. Today is the actualization of all yesterdays, the potentiality of all tomorrows.

Today needs no reason for being. It is its own reason for being. Sufficient that it is today.

Life needs no reason for being. It is its own reason for being. Sufficient that it is life.

You need no reason for being. You are your own reason for being. Sufficient that you are you.

God loves you for what you are, not for what you have done or have not done. What are you? You are His child. That is your reason for being.

You are born a king. What ambition can a king have to become something more than what he already is? He can only aspire to be the best possible king.

It is as if the rose should cry out, "For what was I born?" O Rose, you were born to be a perfect rose! O Man, you were born to be a perfect man of God!

Aim at the highest, though you may not hit it. If you never aim beyond your reach, you will not grow. To be is to grow, and to grow is to aim beyond your reach. Growth is aspiration, and aspiration is the impulse to be what you were born to be.

Life is made for the high aimers. They are the true aimers. It is they who make all growth possible.

O Man, you are the spiritual seed of God! Grow as a tree grows, rising out of yourself as a tree rises out of itself.

A redwood seed is very small to grow into such a gigantic tree. You are more than a redwood tree. For it has height and breadth and depth, but you have other dimensions. You are Mind. You are Spirit.

O Man, you were made to be the perfect man of God!

God said, *Be!*

Grace

Though God, God only, can create,
I till and weed, and then I wait,
And in the thicket of my thought
Bloom flowers that I never wrought.
I stand in wonder and behold
Beauty I never sowed unfold,
Visions of faith, insights of love,
Truths that I had no forethought of.

Somehow there is in me yet more
Than I myself might settle for,
A faith that brings perfection out
Past my own powers. I have no doubt
One day all unexpectedly
The rose of Christ shall bloom in me.

God's Green Plant

Green hallelujahs fill
Valley and plain and hill;
All earth wears green for life.
The air is like a fife;
The sun is like a shout,
Calling the green life out.
I feel life stir in me;
I hear life's challenge, *Be!*
The resurrection seed
Is in me; I have need,
Like a green plant, to press
Toward greater livingness;
To put forth branch and root,
Till Christ shall be the fruit.

Cygnet

Though I have striven long and strained
For many a goal I have not gained,
One prayer is all I make—that I
May never cease from aiming high;
May I be made of sterner stuff
Than is content with good enough.

It matters not what I have been;
I have capacities within
Me that I have not called upon.
I am God's cygnet, oh, the swan
Of Christ! And I shall find in me
Invincible serenity.

Stamped on my heart is the impress
Of heaven—shall I aim at less?

O Lord Whose Very Name
Is Love

Jesus Savior, little stranger,
You were cradled in a manger.
Could it be, then, as You grew,
There were no questionings in You?
Did You have no thoughts like me,
No doubts of Your divinity?
Feel no inward ache to know?
Never have the need to grow?
When You went to pray apart,
Was it with no puzzled heart?
O Lord whose very name is love
Made flesh, O incarnation of
Infinite compassion, can
You, being God, be less than man?
You had no splendor like a king's.
I see You in the least of things;
I see You shining through man's tears,
Through his uncertainties and fears.
O Holy Infant, little stranger,
Here is my heart—be it Your manger!

"Whom My Soul Loveth"

"Whom My Soul Loveth"

"I will rise now, and go about the city;
In the streets and in the broad ways
I will seek him whom my soul loveth."

I have sought God in the streets of
the world, in men, and in my own soul.
Have I seen Him?

I have seen snow falling, the spring
green pushing upward, the summer
flowers, the grain yellow in the autumn
fields, the fruit burdening the orchards.
I have felt the glory of the sun. I have
heard the feet of the rain running among
the leaves. I have listened to the conver-
sation of ancient trees. Night after night
I have watched the steadfast stars and
ever-changing moon. The redbird has
wakened me, and I have fallen asleep to
the crickets' tune. The majesty of mountains, the wonder of the sea, the stretch
of valleys, the flight of the sky—all these
I have seen.

Are these God? No, but they are the
garments of God.

I have felt the wonder of life, its patient experimenting, its outward, upward striving, its eternal unfoldment. I have heard the laughter of children. I have seen the look in a mother's eyes. I have watched lovers strolling hand in hand and heart in heart. I have known men brave enough to die for one another and selfless enough to live for one another. I have felt what a wonderful thing it is to be a human being.

Is this God? No, but it is the personality of God.

I have been alone under the sky when suddenly I was one with all the beauty and wonder and glory of the world. The sky was not high enough, the horizons were not wide enough to hold my heart. I reached out through all the galaxies and nebulae, the infinite stretches of space, and I knew that they were in me and of me.

I have walked down a street crowded with strangers when suddenly they were not strangers and I felt myself expand and take them in. I felt their loneliest longings, their loftiest aspirations, their hopes and fears, their love and faith and joy. I was the self that transcends self, the larger self that is not bound by space and time, the self that knows that it is one with the reality in all people.

I have gone into a quiet room, shut the doors of the senses, and turned within, and found the peace that passes understanding, the stillness that is the very heart of stillness, the place where there is nothing at all yet I am one with all that is.

Is this God? No, but it is the presence of God.

Where is God?

Search for Him through the crowded city streets. Seek Him in the peaceful countryside. Penetrate into the nucleus of the atom. Follow the curve of emptiness. Go to the end of time. He will be there. Wherever you are, God is.

Know, you who seek Him, that He seeks you more steadfastly. He seeks you. He loves you. He will not leave you alone. You could not walk alone, not for a moment, not in the darkest night. Though you stretched not out your hand, yet your hand would be in His. Though you held not out your heart, yet His heart would infold you.

"I am sought of *them* that asked not for me; I am found of *them that* sought me not."

What is God? Can the eternal be less than infinite? God is the infinite livingness of life that is in all and through all and under all, ever seeking to express itself.

Some seek to catch God in a net of words, but God is more than a word. He is more than any thought that a man's mind can hold, yet He is the least thought that springs there. He is the first cry uttered by a newborn child, yet He is more than all the utterances of all the theologians.

God is more than all thought, all feeling, and all vision. He is the life that reveals that there is no death. He is the love that transforms hate into constructive energy. He is the intelligence that lifts ignorance into an understanding of Himself, of human beings, and of the universe.

O child of God, He is the truth of your own being!

I Am in God's Heart

Sometimes I know that I am in God's
    heart;
Sometimes I feel alone,
But always when my thoughts and I grow
    still
I know that I am part
Of Being, and I serve a kindlier will
And have a larger purpose than my own;
Somehow I sense
Through all the mischance of my life's
    events
The working out of good I never
    planned—
I must be in God's heart, being in His
    hand.

And though I have not seen Him face to
    face,
Because I know God is
In my heart, I can trust I am in His.
I am no fragment of
Existence, set adrift in time and space;
I am the heartbeat of eternity—
I am caught up into the Heart of Love
Because I have a heart of love in me.

Inmost in Us

Inmost in us, Father, and farthermost,
Lord of forever, keeper of the far,
Ruler and rule beyond the farthest star
Yet nearer to us than this flesh we trust,
Our flesh Your house, our mind Your
    form, the world
Your word, infinity around You furled;
Not far from us, no farther than a
    thought,
Lord of our heart and heaven, who made
    all
And know each faltering, each sparrow-
    fall,
Who sought and found us, though You
    were unsought,
Who heard our cry before it was a cry,
Nearer than the need and every need's
    supply,
Who are the whole, indwelling every
    part—
O Father love, You have us in Your heart!

Loveliness Like Spring's

In the economy of things,
What need for loveliness like spring's?
What possible use for a rainbow? Why
Should stuff become a butterfly?
The dogwood did not have to look
Like something from a fairy book—
The dogwood merely is a tree;
Likewise, a sunset or a sea
Would serve as well if it were plain;
What has a singing bird to gain
That it should make my heart leap up?
What a waste of gold on a buttercup!

What made the world we may not know,
But whatever conceived sunlight and snow
And leaves for fall and stars for night,
We may have faith, has made things right.

Sea Voice

The crying of the gull, the channel bell,
The surf, the wind—the sea's voice is in
    these;
What truth is the sea saying? Who can
    tell
Save him who has a spirit like the sea's?

The deep calls to the deep. The boundless
    sea
Speaks to the boundlessness that is in you.
The sea, the trumpet of infinity,
Cries that the Infinite is in you, too.

O mariner for God, beyond the shore
Of self are seas not marked in any chart,
Deeps of the spirit never dared before,
A new dimension for your landlocked
    heart.

It is not only wind and surf you hear,
The Infinite is thundering in your ear.

"A Little Lower than the Angels"

"A Little Lower than the Angels"

"What is man, that thou art mindful of him? and the son of man, that thou visitest him? For thou hast made him a little lower than the angels, and hast crowned him with glory and honor."

Standing on the shore of an inlet, you may see only a small and agitated stretch of water. You cannot guess at the deeps, the wonders, the boundless extent, the meaning of the sea. Absorbed in the little deeds of every day, the commonplace duties, the momentary needs, you may not see the true meaning of life.

Do you understand how important you are?

You are a special creation of God, and only in you can God fulfill Himself. You are a living soul, original and unique, wonderful and strange.

Do you think that the wind-tossed, cloud-piled sky is vast and moving? Your life is no less vast and moving. Do you think that the sun is splendid and necessary? You are as splendid. You are as necessary.

Do you appreciate the wonder of your own body? Wonderful are your eyes that see and your ears that hear, apprehending shapes and colors, nearness and farness, silence and sound. Wonderful is the stubborn strength of your bones, the clean beauty of your limbs, the dexterity of your hands. Wonderful is the way of a thought in the mazes of the brain and the way of the blood in its vessels. Wonderful is the way of the breath that fans the fires of life. Wonderful is the way of food that is transformed into living cells. Wonderful is the way of the healing power that can restore its own tissues. Wonderful is the way of creative life that can fashion out of the substance of itself a new body for a living soul.

Do you appreciate the wonder of your own mind? With your mind you can create beauty and you can seek truth. You can dream dreams of perfection. You can feel the divine discontent that is the human mark. You can dare. You can persevere. You can recall the past.

You can plan the future. You can soar beyond the farthest mist of stars. You can explore the atom. You can go alone into the aloneness of yourself. You can mount up with prayer toward God. You can shape tools and acquire knowledge. You can gain dominion over the external universe. You can achieve the mastery of yourself.

Do you appreciate the wonder of your own Spirit? Do you know that you are one with the living God? You are one with the God who fashioned the physical universe, the simplest secrets of whose construction our wisest physicists are only now discovering. You are one with the God who in the laboratory of a living cell effortlessly creates substances that all our chemists in acres of factories cannot duplicate. You are one with the God who fashioned the human soul and made it so wonderful and strange that even you who possess it cannot see its full extent or meaning. You are one with the God who made life, and made it so interesting that He Himself enjoys the living of it. As the leaves are a part of the tree, as the sands are a part of the earth, as the cells of your body are a part of you, so you are a part of the Spirit of God.

Out of itself the sea advances in a wave. Out of themselves the heavens form the shifting cloud. Out of itself the Spirit of life unfolds the endless variety of living things. You are the crest of the wave and the shape of the cloud and the human form called you. But you are also the force of the sea, the movement of the heavens, the Spirit of life.

O threefold wonder, infinite creation of the Infinite, know how wonderful you are! All the forces of life and the universe have operated eternally to produce you. There is no atom anywhere but has had its effect upon you, and you have had your effect upon them all.

Life has a purpose and a meaning, and looking through its transitory forms, we can perceive its underlying unity. Your life is a pattern, a part of a larger whole, and you are an eternal soul. Even the troubles that come like clouds and storms have a meaning and are part of the pattern.

You are the divine inhabitant of body and mind, eternal adventurer through time and space, through chance and change. Before you were born, you had come through an eternity of experiences. You have an eternity before you yet. You are exploring the unknown. You are bringing form to the unformed. Feeling fear, you have come forward with courage. In spite of selfishness, you have aspired to love. Having doubts, you have dared to seek the truth.

Have you never won great victories or heard your name shouted in praise? Every moment you live is a victory. O spiritual pioneer, to live well is to win the greatest victory of all! It is not only in high places and on great occasions for kings and conquerors of the world that life's triumphing trumpets sound. They sound in the heart. Listen and you may hear the clear and certain call!

You are a god and the child of God. You are an original creation of the Spirit of life. You are God in the likeness of a man. Eternal light-bringer, you are yourself the light!

Growth

A boy must grow to be a man
Slow inch by inch, thought span by span;
His limbs must find a bolder length,
His heart new tenderness and strength,
His mind must stretch, his muscles fill,
His sinews toughen, and his will.
Life does not leave a boy content
With being less than he was meant
To be; the urge to grow is strong.
He cannot stay a boy for long:
There is in his bones an urge to grow,
There is in his brain a need to know,
There is a pattern in his heart,
A dim perfection he must start
To mount toward, willingly or loath;
For the spirit in man was made for growth.
By ways our wisdom could not plan
The boy in us becomes the man.

River

What is a river? That am I.
But who can say what rivers are?
Am I the water flowing by?
Am I the near bank and the far?

You chart my depth and breadth and course
And find about me nothing strange—
But I say, rivers are more force
Than fact, are everlasting change.

Though your description and your name
May fit me now, I shall not stay
Even a moment hence the same—
I am already on my way.

Out of the infinite, a flow
Of life across infinity,
Into the infinite, I go
How like a river to the sea.

Spring Does Not Wait upon the Heart

Spring has no almanac or chart
To say when grief and winter go.
Spring does not wait upon the heart;
It would bring back its beauty though
It were unseen; the singing bird
Would sing if it were never heard.

Why should we hug last winter's grief
When every leaf unfolds and grows?
Have we less faith than a frail leaf?
Now the least clod foretells a rose—
Have we less courage than a clod?
Good people, we are sons of God!

Prayer Is Life

Prayer Is Life

I have made many kinds of prayer, almost wordless prayers of spiritual anguish, and formal prayers learned by rote. I have prayed on waking in the morning, in the evening as I have fallen asleep, and at special times I have set aside by day. I have joined in prayer with others, said grace at meals, recited psalms in church. Waking at night, I have prayed alone. In my times of deepest need I have prayed, and I have prayed when I had no need except to feel at one with God—though this may be the deepest need of all.

Prayer has meant so much to me that I have wondered how those who do not pray are sometimes able to survive. What do they do when there is nothing they can do?

Prayer is survival power. Though the night may come down dark around and the faith with which we face the night seem small, perhaps no faith at all; yet, if we pray, always some spark leaps up through the tinder of our hearts, a little light to show us our way. Prayer is life.

Prayer is a reaching, and every act of prayer stretches the soul. Prayer is spiritual exercise.

There are many ways to pray, as there are many ways to God. The way of the bird is not the way of the fish. The way of the babe is not the way of the man. The way of the beginner is not the way of the master. Yet there is no atom of creation that does not have access to God. Each soul finds its way to Him at the level of its own experience.

For some, prayer is thought; and for some, it is feeling too inarticulate for thought to express. Communion with nature may be prayer, or the enjoyment of art and poetry and music. An act of kindness may be a prayer, a smile, a friendly hand. Work is often a prayer, for work is an affirmation of creative power. Praise is a kind of prayer. So is zeal. There is the prayer that is the distillation of a moment, passionate and intense, and the prayer that is the whole life of a man, the living prayer of what one is.

There is a prayer that is words, and a

prayer that is silence. To rise, the eagle sometimes has to drive with all its pinioned power; and sometimes, launching itself on an updraft of air, it has only to spread its wings and float serene in order to be borne aloft.

Sometimes when I pray I pray aloud. To control my thinking, I must often phrase my thoughts in words and speak the words aloud or even write them down. My thoughts may be likened to horses, milling in my mind, racing this way and that; but words put a bridle on them and enable me to direct them. So I often have to affirm words of Truth over and over in order to direct my thought Godward.

Yet, sometimes when I pray I do not need to speak any word at all. I merely need to turn my thought to God, and the thought of God floods my mind. I merely need to give myself to God, and God gives Himself to me.

Much of prayer is speaking, yet much of it is listening. And the speaking we do in prayer is important, but the listening is even more important. For it is as we listen that God speaks. And it is when we are still that God acts. It is in the silence that the word of God is uttered and the work of God is done.

Some wonder how they will recognize the word of God. I know only that when God speaks it is in a language you will understand. If it is words, it will be words you know. If it is feelings, you will understand them, too. For feeling is the unforgotten language of the heart; you could speak it before you learned words, the language of the mind.

There is a prayer that asks for things and a prayer that asks for thoughts, and there is a prayer that asks for nothing but gives all. I have prayed for many things. I have cried aloud for help; I have wheedled and bargained and demanded —but what have I ever really prayed for except to know that I am a child of God? I have seen the beautiful bird of Truth fly overhead and would hold it in my heart.

I would know God and understand my relation to Him, and I would know Him and know myself, not with an intellectual knowing, but in every fiber of my mind and heart. And this is why I pray.

For this is a knowing that does not

come from study, but only from prayer. There are many kinds of knowing. Sometimes the mind studies life as it studies a book; it skims over the surface and absorbs not life, but words, which it calls life.

It is one thing to read a book on aerodynamics; it is another thing to fly. As a bird knows flight by flying, I would know life by living. And I would know God, not as a word, but as a living presence in my life.

I am the green plant of God, and I would know Him as the leaves of a tree know sunlight. I would absorb Him and be absorbed in Him. I would make His substance mine and His life mine so that I can make my life and substance His. I would use Him to be used by Him.

This is why I pray.

Many times when I have prayed for things, I have not got what I prayed for, yet I feel I have never prayed in vain.

Perhaps things have not changed as I have wished them to change, but always I have changed. Always some change is wrought by prayer, sometimes in the fabric of things, always in the fabric of self.

Then, too, I have a sense that my life is more than I have power to see or foresee.

Columbus was disappointed in his search for India—and discovered a new world! I, too, have been disappointed in this or that—and have discovered new worlds. My own self is such a world. God is such a world.

Prayer is a journey we make into ourselves, a journey we make toward God. We think of ourselves as islands, but we are truly mainlands. Beyond the cape of self lies a continent of being. It is not to our changing mortal self that we must look to understand our meaning and our destiny, but to this larger selflessness that lies beyond. "For this corruptible must put on incorruption, and this mortal must put on immortality."

The highest prayer is not the one that asks for things, but the one that seeks a sense of God and our relation to Him, a sense of our abiding in the hands of God, in the love of God.

The prayer that is answered is the prayer of the whole human being. What our whole being demands—this is what

52

we always receive from life; it may or may not be what we cry out for in a moment of pain or desire.

This is why prayer often works in great needs more readily than in trivial ones. A great need focuses the whole of us, whets us, as it were, to a razor edge of faith that nothing can resist.

Prayer is the marshaling of all our faculties. It is a unifying force. Sometimes we feel like "splinter" people, lonely and alone. We cannot read our direction right. But prayer orients us. It unifies us with ourselves and makes us whole. It unifies us with life and makes us alive. It unifies us with God.

Prayer is not for the purpose of changing things but of changing us. It is not to make the Infinite conform to our will but to help us to understand and conform to the will of the Infinite. Shall I change the sea by shouting or the wind by wailing? Yet when I was a child I dug a hole in the sand; and even as I dug, the sea welled into the hole and filled it full. When I pray I dig down through the sands of self, so that the sea of God may fill me full.

I do not pray to change God. How

would I change the wholly good? The breeze of God blows steady all the time; I pray so that I may avail myself of it.

It is not God but I who need to change. This is why I use affirmative prayer.

At the center of things there is a harmonious will. This will is life; this will is joy; this will is order; this will is love. Affirmative prayer harmonizes us with this central will of being.

This is affirmative prayer—to know in the face of sickness that underneath are the everlasting arms of wholeness and in the truest part of us we are inseparably one with life; to be able to hear through the discords of daily living the music of immortal love and to strike its chords from the key of our own being; to be able to look at lack, yet to drink deep from unseen wells of plenty. It is the ability to see the facts and flaws, yet know that they are not reality.

True prayer is apprehension of the changeless Truth, which abides at the heart of the changeful world, the Truth of life and joy and order and love, the Truth of God.

For myself, I have not found the meaning and value of prayer to lie so much in the answer to prayer as in the prayer itself. For prayer is a way of life as well as a way of facing life. It is an end as well as a means. It is a spiritual experience.

Prayer is the way of walking with God instead of walking alone. Those who have a habit of prayer are never far from God, even though at times they may lose sight of Him.

Because they have the habit of prayer, they often find things changed by their prayers. But even when things do not change they have a sense that all is well. For they have a sense of a sustaining presence—at the heart of things, compassion!

Though they may not understand why some things occur, they know that God is there. Therefore, nothing that occurs can be meaningless. They and their lives are meaningful.

So they can accept their lives and themselves, striving to change what they feel is good to change, but accepting what they cannot change in the faith that behind all the events of life God is working out His pattern of divinity.

To those who pray, prayer is life itself!

My Miracle

Why must I seek forever for a sign
Instead of looking for the light within?
It is not in the skies the light will shine
But in myself God's glimmer will begin
And grow. If I would find Him let me
   seek
Not vainly for strange visions, but in me.
I shall not hear His voice unless I speak
Kind words; I shall not see Him till I see
Him in the small, unnoticed, everyday
Good deeds of a good life; I shall not find
My miracle in any other way
Save by the transformation of my mind.

Mind's Millpond

How welcome is the pause of prayer,
When all my rushing thoughts descend
Suddenly toward a silence, where
Turmoil and turbulency end

In a deep inward quietness—
My thoughts race thither and are still.
Prayer is mind's millpond, whence I press
Forth with fresh power to turn life's mill.

Homeward

Home the shepherd and the sheep
Come at evening from the hill,
Through a silence kind and deep,
Full of shadows soft and still.
Still and soft and deep and kind
The gentle blessing of a prayer
Falls like evening on the mind.
Homeward from the hills of care
Now my thoughts return like sheep.
I shall pray and pray until
Peace comes dropping down like sleep,
And I am home, and I am still.

Fragile Things

How fragile is a flower!
It may not last an hour;
Even more fragile are imaginings.

Yet thoughts and flowers both
Possess the gift of growth.
I wonder at the strength of fragile things:

On a harsh peak, where rock
Is shattered by the shock
Of wind and frost, a fragile flower survives

And one Christ-centered thought,
Too tenuous to be caught,
Alters the whole direction of our lives.

Thought Is a Solitude

An unfrequented country road may be
The good companion of an afternoon;
Nature is often pleasant company,
Even when our own thoughts are out of
    tune.

And sometimes when there is nobody near
To walk with or to talk with, we are less
Alone than with the friends who hold us
    dear;
Being alone need not be loneliness,

For sometimes when we go alone and shun
The world of men awhile, we grow aware
Of the compassion that makes all things
    one.
Thought is a solitude, and so is prayer.

And it is only when we draw apart
That we are drawn close to life's secret
    heart.

"Help Thou Mine Unbelief"

"Help Thou Mine Unbelief"

"Lord, I believe; help thou mine unbelief." Out of how many troubled hearts this cry has risen!

For some it is easy to believe. To them God is as real as their own hands or eyes; His purposes are plain, His love is sure. They may not be able to put their faith into words. They do not need to. They have it in their heart, and they put it into all they say and do.

For others it is not easy to believe. They want to believe. They pore over books of metaphysics and study the teachings of mystics and saints. They spend long hours in prayer. Yet they lack a heart of faith. Even after years the mists of doubt remain, the weary cry still rises: "Help thou mine unbelief."

Faith is the foundation of religion. Psychologists analyze its nature. Mystics describe its effects. Theologians dispute its meaning. When we hear of miracles, we hear that they were wrought through faith. When we pray and do not get what we pray for, we are likely to be told that we do not have enough faith.

What is this faith that we are told is so important to us?

Faith is not so much a matter of the mind as of the heart. Sometimes in seeking to understand God as a principle, we lose sight of Him as a presence. Theologians and philosophers can know God as words to set down in books, but a child that cannot even utter the name of God may have a faith beyond that of learned priests. To have faith is not to theorize about God or even to imagine Him, but to experience Him.

Faith is the opposite of fear. Have you ever felt the icy feet, the racing heart, the unnerved hands of fear? The hands of faith are strong and sure. The feet of faith move steady to the will. The heart of faith beats quietly in tune with God. Faith is a warmth, a feeling of well-being that envelops the body and overflows the mind. Faith brings an inward peace, a tranquil spirit.

Faith is the expectation of the unexpected. Faith is an open and courageous heart. The arms of faith are outstretched, not in supplication but in surrender to life's sovereign will, in submission to the ruling order of the universe, in receptivity to good.

Faith is the power to see in the disappointment of today the fulfillment of tomorrow, in the end of old hopes the beginning of new life. Faith is the inward power to see beyond the outward signs, the power to know that all is right when everything looks wrong.

When our fondest dreams seem to go amiss and our dearest prayers seem to remain unanswered, faith is a vision of life that soars beyond the limitations of the self—these narrow senses, this imperfect reason, this drift of circumstance—and sees that our life is a part of something more than we have ever understood, that in spite of all that may seem and all that may happen there is an ultimate fulfillment, that all is well, that all must be well; for life has an eternal meaning, we are one with the infinite, and whatever may befall us, in the all-infolding, all-unfolding everness of God it will work out for good.

To have such faith is to have the serenity of the saint, the passion of the poet, and the exaltation of the mystic.

You can learn to have faith.

Faith is not an abstraction; it is an attitude toward life, a feeling about life. It does not come out of signs or miracles or any outward happenings so much as out of inward growth.

If you cannot believe in much, then believe in the little that you can. Start where you are and grow. What seed can have a foreknowledge of the tree it will become? What thorny bush can prophesy the rose? What worm can tell of the butterfly? Faith grows.

If you find yourself deploring how little your faith is, think how far you have come with the little faith you have. As you climb a hill it is sometimes well to look back to see how far you have come instead of always looking at the interminable heights ahead.

Sometimes you may have more faith than you imagine, and when you need it you will find it there within you.

Have you never, standing by the sea or walking down a country road or wandering through a field or wood or gazing at the starry sky, suddenly been lifted up and out of yourself, overwhelmed by beauty, so that for a moment you were not anything at all, but were a part of all that is? Surely this is faith.

Have you never stood on a busy corner and felt your heart go out, clear out, to the people, all the people, your people, feeling their minds all winged with dreams like yours, feeling their hearts all big with yearnings like yours, feeling the human tide of life moving, ceaselessly moving, moving forward? Surely this is faith.

Have you never in the silence of yourself felt a sense of being more than self? Surely this is faith.

Faith grows.

And the faith that grows out of questioning is stronger than the faith born of blind acceptance. It can withstand the shocks of circumstance. Only he who questions the universe and questions it in utter honesty can grow in his comprehension of the truth.

Sometimes when a man has much to meet he doubts his power to meet it. He feels alone. Yet if he but keeps on, he will not fail, he cannot fail—even if he falters, even if he falls. Even in defeat he is victorious; for he wins the greatest victory of all, victory over himself.

This is certain; he is not alone. He is one with the sovereign and sustaining will, one with the abiding order, one with the goodness and the heroism, one with the upward urge, one with the triumphant spirit of life.

Though there be no shouts of praise, no laurels, he bears the whole race forward in his great stride, and the compassion that infolds the world catches him to itself and presses him even into the inmost heart of life, even into the love of God Himself.

"Lord, I believe; help thou mine unbelief."

When from your heart the troubled cry goes up, know that there is no cry but that somehow there is an answer. There is a love. There is a power. There is a wisdom, and there is a way to go. Let your heart hold fast; the way will be made plain.

Mountains Affirm

Mountains have sun-crowned slopes and
    wear snow's white;
There is a grandeur in their untrod height;
They stand as firm as faith, yet soar like
    prayer.
Mountains are affirmations. They declare
The absolute and have a power to bless
My spirit with infolding quietness.
Mountains remind me that I have in me
An untouched summit of serenity,
Abiding, crowned with majesty, untrod,
Upsoaring. Mountains make me think of
    God.

As Still as Snow

It is not hard to be aware
When all goes well that God is there;
But in my winter moments, when
Doubts buffet my bare spirit, then
It is that I must find God real.

And it is then I pray and feel
God's peace upon my mind come down
Like nightfall on a noisy town,
God's love upon my heart as still
As snow upon a winter hill.

Rock of Reassurance

Our hearts need reassurance like a rock
To steady us at times against the tide
And give us sanctuary from time's shock,
But of what rock shall we say, "This will
    abide"?

Basalt and granite can be swept away,
There is not any rock that I know of
That is unfailing refuge and sure stay
Except the heart's assurance of God's love.

The heart that knows God's love shall it-
    self become
A rock of reassurance, God's holy hill;
For time and tide cannot separate it from
Its faith in the sure outworking of His
    will.

My Heart Is Like a Mountain Stream

My heart is like a mountain stream
Skipping upon the hills and under
Dark cliffsides, glint of sun and gleam
Of foam, a music and a thunder.

Like a bubbling joy a child runs after,
Welling up like hope, like love, like
    wonder,
Eternal change, eternal laughter—
O magic flute, O foam flowers flinging!

Through glens of gloom my heartstream
    breaks
Like light to start far echoes ringing—
Falling upon life's rocks, it makes
A mightier music, sweeter singing.

The Heart Will Find Its Own

The Heart Will Find Its Own

How sweet are the syllables that signify love! Heart has no deeper longing than to utter or hear uttered the words "I love you!" They are like the sight of land to a sailor long adrift.

We pursue many ends—power and pleasure, riches and knowledge, health and fame—and they are worthy ends, but without love they are little more than a child's toys.

Without love this existence is life imprisonment. Until love sets us free, each of us is confined in the narrow prison of himself. Who has never felt that he is bound as by walls? Love bursts these walls of self and selfishness.

We seek and do not know what it is that we seek. Yet often a word would fill the emptiness, a touch would ease the ache. How little of love it takes to make a house of happiness out of a lonely heart!

We have seen love: in the look of a

young man and woman; in the fingers of a mother fondling her baby; in the clasped hands of friends; in the bent back of an old priest bowed in the service of God; in the eyes of a student poring over treasured volumes; in the faces of soldiers marching in the ranks of hate; in the patience of a biologist peering through his microscope; in the beauty and order of the universe that are the signs of God's love for us.

What is love?

To understand love, as to understand God, one must experience it. Some seek popularity believing that this approval of people in general is love, but love is more than popularity. Others seek prestige believing that this is love, but love is more than prestige.

For above all love is a sharing. Love is a power. Love is a change that takes place in our own heart. Sometimes it may change others, but always it changes us.

To love is to find happiness in making others happy. It is to understand what others think and feel and need. It is to say and do the things that make them eager to be with us; and to do these things not for effect but because it is natural for us to do them.

It is to know the imperfections of others yet see them perfect.

It is to know their weaknesses yet see them strong, and because of our vision and our faith to make them stronger than they are.

It is to accept others as they are; and when they fail our aspirations for them or spurn our outstretched hand, to keep open the door of our heart.

It is to appreciate the importance of others and to help them appreciate their own importance.

It is to grow into the heart of others and to become a part of their life yet not bind their heart nor limit their life.

It is to lose ourself in something greater than ourself, as a small spark loses itself in other sparks and becomes a star.

There is no unworthy love. The object of love may be unworthy. But love is the supreme beauty, the final joy. Even if sorrow comes with love, love makes us able to meet it and transfigure it, to rise through it as we could not have done had we never loved.

When we are in love—with an idea, a person, people, God—we walk upon the pinnacles of life. We are lifted out of ourselves and become something more than we have ever been before.

Some are afraid to love, afraid lest their love be unreturned, afraid lest someone catch a glimpse behind their careful mask. It is true that love will lift the mask—but how gentle are the eyes of love! To be afraid to love is to be afraid to live.

Some say that they love God but not men. But how can we love harmony and not music? How can we love light and not the morning? How can we love nature and not the spring? How can we love God and not the likeness of God, which is man?

When some feel that they have love, they have only a word. It is easy to say that we love strangers when they are far from us or that we love God when He is but a shadowy abstraction. But when the stranger knocks at our heart and cries, "Share!"—when God becomes the disturber in our soul who answers, "Serve!"—then we find out if we truly love.

Some want to love but do not know how. They are like children who wish to make music but have not mastered any instrument. They have not learned; but one can learn to love. The beginning of love is giving.

For him who has never given it is not easy to give. Let him begin by giving but a little. Let him give a smile where he would have passed unheeding. Let him give a kind word where he would not have spoken.

If you will take one faltering step, love will rush to meet you and bear you on. For love is the great giver.

Do you wish to find yourself? You must lose yourself. Do you wish to be the master of life? You must be its servant. Do you wish to receive love? You must give it.

Receiving is a pleasure, but giving is life itself. It is only by giving self away that a person grows.

The mind that withholds its wisdom, the strength that refuses the burden is like a wasteland, sterile and meaningless. It is not because it never receives fresh supplies of water but because it has no outlet that the Dead Sea is dead. If the sun should stop giving its light, it would become only another dead star.

We may be a chaos or a cosmos. We may succumb to hate and death or rise to love and life. Love is mightier than hate. Life is stronger than death. To learn to love is to learn the secret of life.

There is a power that links the earth and sun and binds the stars together into galaxies, a power that binds the segments of life into a perfect whole. Alone in our little self, we feel our incompleteness. We know in our heart that we are a part of something more.

Love is the power that links the lonely islands of men's souls, beaten by icy separating seas of ignorance and fear and circumstance. Love is the power that links us all in God, as all the islands are linked in the earth. Yet love is not a chain. Love is completion.

The river runs into the sea, and its waters mingle with the waters of the sea. The sea is not the river and the river is not the sea. Yet who can separate one from the other?

O God of love, You are the sea and we

are a river flowing to the sea! Who shall say which is the river and which is the sea?

You are a flame and we are steel tempered in the flame. Who shall say which is the steel and which is the flame?

You are fulfillment and we are desire. Who shall say which is the desire and which is the fulfillment?

You are spirit and we are flesh. Who shall say which is the flesh and which is the spirit?

For this is the mystery and miracle of love, that we are separate yet we are one! And the heart, though it must overleap eternity, will find its own.

Love's Omnipotence

Sometimes I think how little I know me.
I am the unexplored, for the most part;
I stand, as it were, on the edge of a wide
    sea,
And the sea I gaze upon is my own heart.

For I have other dimensions and am more
Than I have judged I was from surface
    seeing;
This face, this body—these are but the
    shore;
How far beyond them stretch my seas of
    being!

I have thought I was an island, a rocky
    shelf
Of separateness, but the eternal deep
Forever breaks across my reefs of self.
In me and over me and through me sweep

The seas of God, and often now I sense
That I am one with love's omnipotence.

The Shepherd

Shepherd of hearts, we are Your sheep.
Ah, Christ, what meadows are as fair
As faith? What waters run as deep
As the still spirit given to prayer?

Upon the lilies of Your love
Our hungering hearts are daily fed,
And nightly in the pastures of
Compassion You prepare our bed.

Even the tiger in the breast,
That has no terror of the rod,
Subdued by love lies down to rest
With the forgiving lamb of God.

Morning Carol

On a spring morning, like a child
That loves all creatures great and small,
I feel akin and kind to all
The little creatures of the wild.
With every bounding lamb I leap
Up through the flesh in which I sleep;
I hear the hidden field mouse cry;
I feel the heartbeat of the hare;
And no bird rises on the air
But I put forth my wings and fly;
Nothing that lives but we are one.
God came to me and called me son;
My Lord Christ came and called me
    brother.
Small creatures of the field and wood,
You are part of our brotherhood—
We are all one with one another.

Another Dawn

Another Dawn

Faced with the passing of someone we love, our heart cries out in the passion of its loneliness and is not comforted with easy answers.

Our heart tells us that we are meant to live, not to die. We are meant to express life ever more consummately. When someone fails to do this, we wonder why.

To understand the meaning of death, we must understand the meaning of life. Looking at life, we see that all things change. But although all things change, nothing perishes. Things only change.

If this is true in the world of things, how much more true it is in the world of mind! Soul has a substance of its own, no less permanent for being immaterial, no less real for being invisible. We cannot measure it with calipers or weigh it in a balance. We cannot feel it with our fingers or see it with our eyes. But it is there, substantial, real. It changes, but it will not perish.

Life does not begin with birth. It does not end with death. Life is an eternal process, an eternal progress. This visible form, this audible voice, this aggregation of organs, this network of ideas—we are more than these. These are the trappings of visibility. We are an expression of the Spirit of life.

Stand on the shore at night. You can hear the sound of the waves. You can see them break and whiten on the rocks. But the sea itself, vast and imponderable and strange and deep, you cannot see.

The wave breaks on the rocks and then is gone, and all that is left behind is a fading line of foam. Yet the sea is more than the foam that fades on the rock. The sea is more than the wave into which it shaped itself for a moment. When wave and foam are gone the sea abides to shape itself into another wave and fling itself in foam on the rocks again.

You are like a sea that shapes itself into a wave. The wave will expend itself, but you will not expend yourself. You will shape yourself into an infinity of waves. You are the ever-renewing, ever-unfolding expression of infinite life. You are the spirit of the Infinite moving across infinity.

Eternity is not an alternation of life and non-life. There is only life. The truth is that we cannot die. For we are life. Life is energy. Life is expression. It cannot cease because it is ceaselessness. We may change form and vanish from view, but we cannot cease to be. We never cease to be, not for a moment. We cannot be separated from life. We cannot be less than life.

Life is a road that winds among the hills of time. With every turn in the road an old view vanishes, a new view appears. Life is a pilgrimage, a passage through eternity, a journey into the unknown. People are as travelers on a journey.

Some pass quickly beyond the bend in the road that hides them from our view. Some walk beside us all the way. Some seem to creep along, and some pass swiftly as a runner. But life cannot be measured in terms of time, only in terms of living.

When people die they do not cease to be; they only pass beyond human sight.

There is a unity beyond the unities of time and place and even thought, a unity that links us as one, just as all the waves are one sea and all the islands one earth. Does not love link us with our friends though they be on the other side of the earth? So those we love may pass beyond the reach of hands, but not outside the heart.

Why are we afraid of death? It is because we are afraid of the unknown. Yet is not each new day an adventure into the unknown?

Exactly what is on the other side of death we do not know. But we may be sure that it is life. Life is on the other side of death as it is on this side.

Death is not evil. Neither is it good. Is the turning of a page good or evil? Is the rest between two notes of music good or evil? Is the opening of a door good or evil? Death is an incident. It is a part of life, as sleep is a part of life, as nightfall is a part of life. Sleep gives way to waking. Night turns into day. So death is but the passage from life to life.

Death is a door through which we pass into another room. It is a rest between two notes in an unfinished symphony. It is a page we turn to a new chapter in the book of life. It is not the end; it is a new beginning. It is not the fall of night; it is another dawn.

We may not know just what will occur when we pass through the door. Yet we can trust the Keeper of Infinity. Life is the work of a grand and kind intelligence and has an order and a meaning beyond our power to see. Who among us could have planned an atom or a star? Who could have contrived the earth, the seasons, the delicate balance of forces that permits life on earth to exist? What scientist could have fashioned the human body? What philosopher could have thought of the laws that govern mind and space? What poet could have imagined love and wonder?

We can trust this intelligence that made the world. We were not made for dying, or for failure, or for pain. We are meant to live gloriously. We are the children of the Infinite. We have a divine destiny. We are advancing toward this destiny.

Out of the infinite we came and into the infinite we return. But we are upward bound. We have risen through an eternity of experiences. We shall go higher yet.

Now we live in a world of light and darkness, life and death. The sun that rises in the morning seems to set in the evening. Yet, if we could rise out of the shadow of the earth, we should see that the sun does not truly set; it burns in the heavens always. Neither does the sun of life ever set; if we could rise high enough, we should see that life is a continuous process and that death is but the shadow cast by our earthiness.

Though now the appearances of all things change, the laws that rule the world, the insights of love, the wisdom of the heart, the power of faith, of beauty and truth—these do not change. Beyond our day and night, our ebb and flow, our yea and nay, our good and evil, the Eternal is eternally the same.

Let us not be afraid. We are sailors on the sea of eternity, life's wayfarers, and we are well companioned on this voyage. Let us sail on with faith, with courage in our heart. Beyond the dark, behold: It is another dawn!

The Traveler

He has put on invisibility.
Dear Lord, I cannot see—
But this I know, although the road ascends
And passes from my sight,
That there will be no night;
That You will take him gently by the hand
And lead him on
Along the road of life that never ends,
And he will find it is not death but dawn.
I do not doubt that You are there as here,
And You will hold him dear.

Our life did not begin with birth,
It is not of the earth;
And this that we call death, it is no more
Than the opening and closing of a door—
And in Your house how many rooms must
    be
Beyond this one where we rest momently.

Dear Lord, I thank You for the faith that
    frees,
The love that knows it cannot lose its
    own;
The love that, looking through the
    shadows, sees
That You and he and I are ever one!

How Much

How much the human spirit
Outweighs the human pain—
So much that no experience
But can be counted gain!

What faith before impossibles
A man is capable of
Who, being overwhelmed,
Yet trusts that God is love!

What doubter dares to say
Man is not god or near it
When even his defeats become
The triumph of his spirit!

Praise Him!

Praise Him!

How shall I praise my Creator?
Surely by delighting in His works!
Lord, I rejoice in Your world.

Out of what nothingness have You created this wonderful and varied all! I see Your footprint in reality. On every living thing I see the impress of Your hand. In the thoughts that move like winds across my mind I feel Your breath. In every little wish and cry and act of love throughout the world I hear the beating of Your heart.

Dawn is beautiful. No less beautiful is evening. Noon is like a trumpet sounding forth Your glory. Night is like the still benediction of Your peace. Lord, I love Your light and I love Your darkness. I love Your blazing heat and the respite of Your rain. O Lord, I look upon Your works and I cry out, *How wonderful is my Creator!*

I am like a little bird that stretches out his wings in faith, that dances on the invisible air, that sings before the sun has risen in the east. You have given me wings of spirit. You have given me tongues of angels. I shall mount up in my heart singing praises of my Lord.

You have made me, O God, You have made me good. As a priest serves with rejoicing in the temple, I serve You with rejoicing in the temple of my body. I care for it with love, as an incarnation of Your loveliness and life.

I rejoice in my hands. They enable me to do Your work.

I rejoice in my feet. They carry me about Your world.

I rejoice in my eyes. They explore Your wonders.

I rejoice in my ears. They listen for Your word.

In every organ, tissue, nerve, Lord, I rejoice.

Out of a sea foam of cells You have fashioned my body and invested it with iron of spirit and hardihood of heart. Who but You, O Lord, from such fragility could draw such enduring strength?

Lord, I thank You for this flesh. It is Your holy temple.

Lord, I thank You for this world. It is Your seamless robe.

Lord, I thank You for this mind. It is Your living light.

Lord, I thank You for this spirit. It is the likeness of Yourself.

O Lord, how skillfully have You contrived me—with senses that I may delight in Your light, that I may share in the beauty of the world that You have made; with a spirit that I may delight in doing Your will; with a mind and body that I may be as co-creator with You.

You have made me good, even in Your own image. You have made the world good, even out of Your own life, substance, and intelligence.

You have made me heir, joint heir with Jesus Christ, to the riches of Your love, to the riches of Yourself. You have given me richly all things to enjoy. I praise You, O Lord, by living richly.

Not by hating but by loving, not by doubting but by believing, not by casting down but by lifting up, not by denying life but by affirming life, I praise You. Not by condemning but by praising do I praise You.

I praise You not by giving up my good but by giving myself away in love. Oh, that like Christ I might love all humanity! Oh, that like You I might love all the world! that not one star might fall, nay, not one sparrow, but my heart would be there!

I praise You, O Lord, for my heart, which has the God-capacity to love.

I praise You, O Lord, for my mind, which has the God-capacity to think.

I praise You, O Lord, for my body, which has the God-capacity to act.

I praise You, O Lord, for my spirit, which has the God-capacity to be.

I praise You, O Lord, with my world-affirming faith.

How shall I praise my Creator?

Surely by delighting in His works!

A Passing Day

To tell you what today was like
Is more than I can do;
How does God make each passing day
Look different and new?

The birds and I were early up
To meet our friend the sun
And hallelujah him before
The morning had begun.

All men who could came out of doors,
And they looked glad to be
On time's renowned adventure
With earth's bright company.

It would take tongues of angels
To translate into sound
The evidences of God's love
That roundabout I found.

What riches has eternity
That it can give away
Such infinite perfection
To just a passing day!

My Heart Makes Its
Own Weather

My heart makes its own weather,
So let the world grow gray;
My heart starts saying April
When April's far away.

In spite of rain and reason
And winter on the wing,
My heart has its own season,
And my heart says it is spring!

Blow wind and bitter weather,
Come care and whistling cold,
An April heart will never
Grow gray or crabbed or old.

Time is a wrinkled treason;
Age is an old untruth.
Heart, keep your changeless season,
Green April, golden youth!

How Can I Know?

How Can I Know?

How can I know God is? How can I know the world makes sense? How can I know there is a purpose in living? How can I know?

These are the questions of all of us. When we seek for an answer to them, where shall we look?

Look out at the vastness of things. See the stars blossoming like the unfolding petals of a rose, and you sense the moving order that rules the deeps of space. Look at the least blade of grass—out of sunlight and water and air, it makes new life!—and you sense the inconceivable intelligence that works in the least of things.

And more than intelligence! If we could get at the heart of things, a heart is what we would find, something much more like heart than mind, much more like love than law, much more like beauty than reason.

Take rainbows, for example. The Bible says a rainbow is a token of God's covenant with man. There is a reason for rain, but not for a rainbow. The universe would operate as efficiently without one, only not so beautifully, that is all. Only the Spirit of divine delight could have conceived rainbows, the same Spirit that made butterflies, those flowers with wings! And indeed all the infinite, outpouring, heaped-up, overflowing variety of things bursting the seams of the world makes me know absolutely that something is at work here so alive that life is too weak a word to describe it. The Spirit of God is not just life, not just intelligence. It is sheer exuberance, the love of joy in living! It never makes two blades of grass alike. It crowds every crack with growing things and space with universes.

Clouds form and dissolve, birds sing, insects rise, leaves tremble, flowers unfold—all is change, activity, livingness. You may be part of this livingness. The universe is as a web, beautifully woven, its threads spiraling out, linking every living thing, even every atom, so intimately, so perfectly that no least thread, no least point at the perimeter, can be touched but the whole web vibrates in harmony. You can be one with this oneness of things. You need not be little and alone, isolated and meaningless. You are part of life.

One with life, you lose your sense of separateness, your sense of self. No bird flies, but your thought takes flight; no bird sings, but a song is in your heart. You are brother to the fly and cousin to the cricket. You are as much a part of life as a cloud is part of the air. Who shall say where cloud ends and air begins? At its edges it is some of both. At your edges you are part of all that is, part of the livingness of life.

In the infinite flux of life, there is no separateness, there is only wholeness, only the many faces of the One. Give yourself to living, and you will find meaning, for you will be one with the One life.

Where shall you look to see God?

Look at yourself. Do you see a mortal, flesh-and-blood creature? That is not what I see when I look at you. I see a spiritual being. Why do I think you are spiritual? For one thing, because you have to live as if you were.

If we know what makes a creature happy, we know its true nature. To be happy, a swallow must fly. So we say it is a bird of flight. To be happy, a thrush must sing. So we say it is a songbird. To be happy, a man must try to satisfy spiritual desires. What else then can we say save that he is Spirit!

If man were a mortal, flesh-and-blood creature with only physical needs to satisfy, then a life spent in satisfying these needs should be the most satisfactory of lives. But it is the least satisfactory. Something in you is more than flesh-and-blood. Something in you is wings. Something in you is song. Something in you is Spirit.

What are the longings of your heart, the aspirations of your mind? Consider them well, for they reveal the pattern in which you were formed. They are the voice of your true self, demanding expression. For this you were formed before Abraham was! And all the forces of heaven and earth combine to bring this true pattern in you to fruition.

There is something in you that tells you you were meant for more than all you have achieved, no matter what that may be; something in you that will be satisfied with nothing less than greatness. It may settle for less, but it is not satisfied. It may be covered over with years of dusty mediocrity, of compromise and resignation to necessity. But it is there.

Something in you is Spirit, and it hungers and thirsts after spiritual things—after righteousness, usefulness, selflessness. It is not content merely to live; it has to live well!

You are more than body, more than mind. These may be altered, but there is something in you that cannot be altered. It is immortal. It is incorruptible. How do I know that this is there? Because I have caught glimpses of it. I have looked with love's eyes. It is not only when I look at Jesus that I see God. I see God when I look at every person.

Sometimes we think we would believe if only we had a sign. "Give me a revelation, God!" we cry. "O Lord, let pass a miracle!"

This I believe, that anyone who sincerely asks for signs will have signs. Pray, pray steadfastly, and you will have prayers answered.

But do not seek for God to show Himself in supernatural ways and forget that

He is constantly showing Himself in natural ways. He is the unusual, no doubt; but He is the usual, too. Do not seek the burning bush and miss the bushes glowing with bloom in your own backyard. Do not look for Him in the heavens, and pass Him by in your neighbor without speaking.

Do you seek a miracle? What is more a miracle than morning, when the light comes streaming back to earth? Or spring, when death is overcome by every greening clod? A star is a miracle, and you live on one. Thought is a miracle, and it is closest to you of all that is. You are a miracle. Every moment of your life is more packed with miracles than the Bible.

It is all right to ask for signs, but to build on signs is to build on sands, for it is to build on appearances. We have to go deeper than appearances, even good appearances; else the first adversity will sweep our faith away. We cannot build much of a faith on the fact that we happen to be having a comfortable, pain-free existence.

But there is a knowledge of God, there

is a faith in life, that has nothing to do with appearances. For fundamentally God and life are not something we know with our brain, but in our bones, in the very marrow of our bones, the marrow of our spirit. I do not need to convince the hare that bursts from under my feet and bounds breakneck away that life is good. He knows. He may be wet and cold and alone and shelterless and hungry. Yet he knows. Every frantic leap he makes is a living affirmation of life.

The hare knows—and deep down so do we all—that one moment of life is worth infinitely more than all the non-life (if such there could be) in the world. If eternity had no other meaning, it came alive with meaning the moment life appeared in it.

For myself, I have never known with such absolute certainty that God is and life is meaningful and purposive as I knew at a time when appearances were declaring the exact opposite. My brain was full of doubts, but I knew with more than brain. God was there, that is all. Underneath were the everlasting arms. I felt the arms. I recognized the presence.

God was there, that is the only way I can describe what I experienced. At the moment I was deepest down, I was also highest up. I knew Him not by believing in Him or reasoning through to Him. I simply knew Him.

If you want to know the stars, do you study astronomy books? Do you think about stars? Perhaps, but most of all you go out and commune with them, warm and glowing in the dark. And on a dark night when no star appears, the stars may be more meaningful and real than ever. If you live close enough to the stars, they go right on shining in you.

So it is with God. God is not something you have sometimes, if you work hard to find Him. He is in you, and you are in Him.

When you give yourself to life, you have not reasons for living, but life itself. When you give yourself to God, you have not thoughts about God, but God Himself.

How can you know God is? How can you know the world makes sense? How can you know there is a purpose in living? How can you know?

You can know God as you know the stars are shining on a cloudy night, as you know someone you love is in the next room.

Give yourself to life in love and with faith. For then you live not on the surface but at the heart of things. And the heart of things is the heart of God.

Significance

I stood upon a rock and sought
To catch the sea's significance;
There must be some deep truth, I thought,
In such an endless utterance.

But while I stood two children strayed,
Indifferent to the shouting sea,
Upon my rock and laughed and played
Till suddenly it came to me—

The laughter of a child at play,
Passing as fast as foam, means more
Than all the sea can ever say
To the uncomprehending shore.

The human child is frail and small
But in him God has struck His spark,
Which gives significance to all
That else were merely vast and dark.

The Hilltop Heart

If only you have a hilltop heart,
Life's compass points lie far apart;
What heights and deeps life has, how far
The hilltop heart's horizons are!
Hills have a way of stretching minds;
Lured-on imagination winds
Up over crests and down through hollows.
Hills tug at the heart, and the heart fol-
    lows,
Dares the undared, tries the untried.
Hills always have another side;
If you make the climb up and descent,
You may find the valley of content.
Though a hilltop heart may never stand
    still,
Yet the heart was meant for the top of a
    hill!

New Snow

New snow makes new horizons in my
    mind,
Gives me a feeling of the unconfined
Vast sweep of things. The world looks
    twice as wide
With new snow on it. Now on every side
Life stretches beautiful and new and bare,
Mine for the venturing. The snow-sweet
    air
Is joy to breathe; I drink deep of the north
Wind's eagerness. Now all life shouts,
    Step forth!
The little boundaries of yesterday,
The too familiar landmarks on my way,
Have disappeared. The snow is like a new
And brighter revelation of the true
Meaning of life, a vision of untrod,
Untrammeled vistas where I am with God,
The all-infolding All, the Undefined.
New snow is a new outlook in my mind.

I Am There

I Am There

Do you need Me?

I am there.

You cannot see Me, yet I am the light you see by.

You cannot hear Me, yet I speak through your voice.

You cannot feel Me, yet I am the power at work in your hands.

I am at work, though you do not understand My ways.

I am at work, though you do not recognize My works.

I am not strange visions. I am not mysteries.

Only in absolute stillness, beyond self, can you know Me as I am, and then but as a feeling and a faith.

Yet I am there. Yet I hear. Yet I answer.

When you need Me, I am there.

Even if you deny Me, I am there.

Even when you feel most alone, I am there.

Even in your fears, I am there.

Even in your pain, I am there.

I am there when you pray and when you do not pray.

I am in you, and you are in Me.

Only in your mind can you feel separate from Me, for only in your mind are the mists of "yours" and "mine."

Yet only with your mind can you know Me and experience Me.

Empty your heart of empty fears.

When you get yourself out of the way, I am there.

You can of yourself do nothing, but I can do all.

And I am in all.

Though you may not see the good, good is there, for I am there.

I am there because I have to be, because I am.

Only in Me does the world have meaning; only out of Me does the world take form; only because of Me does the world go forward.

I am the law on which the movement of the stars and the growth of living cells are founded.

I am the love that is the law's fulfilling.

I am assurance.
I am peace.
I am oneness.
I am the law that you can live by.
I am the love that you can cling to.
I am your assurance.
I am your peace.
I am one with you.
I am.

Though you fail to find Me, I do not fail you.

Though your faith in Me is unsure, My faith in you never wavers, because I know you, because I love you.

Beloved, I am there.

Deeps

There are deeps in the mind no thought
    has sounded,
Unknown seas of the soul; far-off un-
    rounded
Wild capes of spirit perilous and pounded
By tide and tempest; continents of fact
No voyager has set foot on to send back
Word for the world to follow, where no
    track
Marks the known way; beyond the rim of
    thought
Lie worlds hope charts not, vision has not
    caught,
Uncertain, unimagined, still unsought.

We were not meant for bays and shallows,
    for
Safe sailing never out of sight of shore—
Men, mariners, oh, we were meant for
    more!
Ours are the deeps, the seas we do not
    know,
The seas where none before has dared to
    go,
The seas of faith where only strange
    winds blow.

Leaving known landfalls for the fainter-
    hearted,
To seek the undiscovered, the uncharted—
Where the last voyage ended, there let
    ours be started!

Printed U.S.A.
62-F-7831-25C-6-85